# KINGS AND QUEENS

ELEANOR and HERBERT FARJEON were born in the 1880s into a highly literary family. Eleanor published nearly seventy books, most of which were for children. Together with Herbert, her younger brother, she also wrote a children's pantomime, two operettas and a musical fairy story, *The Glass Slipper*.

ROBIN JACQUES was born in London in 1920. He had no formal art training and was self-taught but went on to illustrate over one hundred books for adults and children, most notably the fairy-tale compilations of Ruth Manning-Sanders. Robin Jacques died in 1995.

# KINGS AND QUEENS

## ELEANOR AND HERBERT FARJEON

*Illustrated by Robin Jacques*

PUFFIN POETRY

PUFFIN BOOKS

UK | USA | Canada | Ireland | Australia
India | New Zealand | South Africa

Puffin Books is part of the Penguin Random House group of companies
whose addresses can be found at global.penguinrandomhouse.com.

puffinbooks.com

First published by J. M. Dent & Sons Ltd 1983
Published in Puffin Books 1987
Published by Jane Nissen Books 2002
Reissued in this edition 2015
001

Text copyright © Gervase Farjeon, 1932, 1940, 1953, 1983
Illustrations copyright © Robin Jacques, 1983
All rights reserved

Set in Baskerville MT
Printed in Great Britain by Clays Ltd, St Ives plc

A CIP catalogue record for this book is available from the British Library

ISBN: 978-0-141-36187-1

www.greenpenguin.co.uk

# Contents

# KINGS AND QUEENS

## *William I*
## 1066

WILLIAM THE FIRST was the first of our kings,
Not counting Ethelreds, Egberts and things,
And he had himself crowned and anointed and blest
In Ten-Sixty-I-Needn't-Tell-You-The-Rest.

But being a Norman, King William the First
By the Saxons he conquered was hated and cursed,
And they planned and they plotted far into the night,
Which William could tell by the candles alight.

Then William decided these rebels to quell
By ringing the Curfew, a sort of a bell,
And if any Saxon was found out of bed
After eight o'clock sharp, it was Off With His Head!

So at BONG NUMBER ONE they all started to run
Like a warren of rabbits upset by a gun;
At BONG NUMBER TWO they were all in a stew,
Flinging cap after tunic and hose after shoe;
At BONG NUMBER THREE they were bare to the knee,
Undoing the doings as quick as could be;
At BONG NUMBER FOUR they were stripped to the core,
And pulling on nightshirts the wrong side before;
At BONG NUMBER FIVE they were looking alive,
And bizzing and buzzing like bees in a hive;

At BONG NUMBER SIX they gave themselves kicks,
Tripping over the rushes to snuff out the wicks;
At BONG NUMBER SEVEN, from Durham to Devon,
They slipped up a prayer to Our Father in Heaven;
And at BONG NUMBER EIGHT it was fatal to wait,
So with hearts beating all at a terrible rate,
In a deuce of a state, I need hardly relate,
They jumped BONG into bed like a bull at a gate.

## William II
### 1087

WILLIAM THE SECOND
He had a red head;
One day to the forest
His huntsmen he led;
A fellow called Tyrrel
An arrow let loose,
And William fell dead
As a Michaelmas goose –
And nobody knows
If the fellow called Tyrrel
Took William's red head
For the king or a squirrel.

## *Henry I*
## 1100

HENRY THE FIRST was a very fine scholar
Who never objected to work;
His writing was neat and his reading a treat,
    And that's why they called him Beauclerk;
But he had a wild son, who in very wild weather
Put forth in a ship, and they went down together –
And though both in French and in Latin he cursed,
What use was his learning to Henry the First?

Henry the First was a very fine scholar,
    And scholars are known to be wise;
He was never in doubt, and he rubbed nothing out,
    And he always knew all the replies;
But his fondness for lampreys he couldn't keep under,
He asked for six helpings one night – so no wonder
If, very soon after, his blood-vessel burst,
Which finished the learning of Henry the First.

# *Stephen*
## 1135

MATILDA claimed the crown
Upon the head of Stephen,
And so they had it up and down
   From morning until even;
The winner now was he,
   And now was she the winner –
Matilda ruled the land at tea,
   And Stephen ruled at dinner.

Matilda claimed the throne
   Her cousin Stephen sat in,
And kept him fighting for his own
   From vesper until matin;
One had the lower hand
   When t'other had the upper –
Till none could tell who ruled the land
   From breakfast-time to supper.

# Henry II
## 1154

HENRY PLANTAGENET
Wherefore do you frown?
There's a priest called Thomas Becket
In Canterbury Town,
And the thought of Thomas Becket
Is worse than the sting
Of a wasp in the bosom
Of Henry the King.

Out on Thomas Becket!
Of yeoman stock he came;
King Henry gave him power,
King Henry gave him fame,
Till the yeoman grew so mighty
The king's heart misgave –
Shall Becket play the master
And Henry the slave?

Ha! Thomas Becket!
'Who,' Henry cried,
'Will rid me of this priest
That's a thorn in my side?'
Then his Four Rough Knights
Rode to Canterbury Town,
And slew Thomas Becket
As the sun went down.

# Richard I
## 1189

TO hew and hack
  The Paynim black,
To flay and fell
The Infidel,
To make short work
Of the murky Turk
And draw the gore
Of the dusky Moor –
This was the first and favourite art
Of Reckless Richard the Lion-Heart,
  Who, sure of aim,
  And never afraid,
  Was always game
  For a good Crusade.

  So he went away
  On the very first day
  He possibly could
  (As they knew he would) –
  Away he went,
  With a nice new tent,
  And a fine black nag,
  And a sleeping bag,
And a shining axe and a gleaming sword,
To batter and scatter the Pagan horde –

And not one jot
Did his zeal abate,
Though England got
In an awful state.

For an absent king
Is bound to bring
His kingdom care
If he's never there –
The laws get mixed,
And the throne un-fixed,
And the national purse
Gets worse and worse,
And the people cry, 'O Richard mine!
Why leave your palace for Palestine?'
So it's better far,
When there's things to do,
To stay where you are,
And see them through.

# *John*
## 1199

JOHN, John, bad King John,
  Shamed the throne that he sat on;
Not a scruple, not a straw,
Cared this monarch for the law;
Promises he daily broke;
None could trust a word he spoke;
So the Barons brought a Deed
Down to rushy Runnymede,
Magna Carta was it hight,
Charter of the People's Right,
Framed and fashioned to correct
Kings who act with disrespect –
And with stern and solemn air,
Pointing to the parchment there,
'Sign! Sign! Sign!' they said,
'Sign, King John, or resign instead!'

John, John, turning pale,
Ground his teeth, and bit his nail;
Chewed his long moustache; and then
Ground and bit and chewed again.
'Plague upon the People!' he
Muttered, 'What are they to me?
Plague upon the Barons, too!'
(Here he had another chew.)
But the Barons, standing by,
Eyed him with a baleful eye;
Not a finger did they lift;
Not an eyelash did they shift;
But with one tremendous roar,
Even louder than before,
*'Sign! Sign! Sign!'* they said.
'SIGN, KING JOHN, OR RESIGN INSTEAD!'
[And King John signed.]

## Henry III
### 1216

HENRY THE THIRD was that poor freak,
A king we speak about as Weak,
And bred in John his father's school
Seemed totally unfit to rule.
So Simon Montfort sternly went
And instituted Parliament.

Had Henry happened to belong
To kings we speak about as Strong,
The House of Commons might have been
A house that nobody has seen,
And we might still be swayed by swords
Instead of by the House of Lords.

# *Edward I*
## 1272

EDWARD THE FIRST was strong and tall,
He had the longest legs of all,
But when from one who wished him harm
A poisoned dagger pierced his arm,
Edward was weak as other men,
His long legs could not help him then.

So Eleanor his gentle wife
Sucked out his wound and saved his life,
And when in time this lady died,
All through England far and wide
He built stone crosses to be seen
In memory of Longshanks' Queen.

## *Edward II*
## 1307

EDWARD THE SECOND
Is commonly reckoned
One of the feeblest of all our kings.
    Favours he lavished on
    Pretty Piers Gaveston,
Giving him duchies and riches and rings.
    This sugar-candified
    Puffed-up and dandified
Man defied all of the Barons with sneers,
    Playing his foolery
    Dressed up in joolery
Sent by King Ned to his Sugar-plum Piers.

    Though Ned was mad about
    This giddy gadabout,
Others had had about all they could bear;
    So the King's favourite
    They made to pay for it
On a fine day for it, spring in the air.
    When those who hated Piers
    Decapitated Piers,
Edward was sorry, but every one said,
    'We executed him
    Seeing it suited him –
Long ere we cut it off, Piers lost his head.'

## *Edward III*
## 1327

WHAT! Haven't you heard
  Of Edward the Third
And his famous French battles?
Don't be so absurd!
Not heard of the foes
Who were mown down in rows
By his archers at Crécy
With arrows and bows?
Not heard of his wife
Who, when there was strife
Round the city of Calais,
Saved many a life,
Because she implored
King Edward, her lord,
To spare the good burghers,
And wasn't ignored?

Not heard of his son? –
I refer to the one
Who was called the Black Prince
And was second to none –
The name that he bore
Was given him for
The favourite suit of
Black armour he wore?

Not heard of the king
Whose glories I sing,
Who built Windsor Castle
Or ordered the thing?
Who tried to get all
Bonnie Scotland in thrall?
Who picked up a garter
One night at a ball?
Don't be so absurd!
Of course you have heard –
*So don't say you haven't –*
Of Edward the Third!

## *Richard II*
## 1377

BEND down your head,
King Richard the Second!
Bend down your head
And put on the crown!
The people are singing
*Good luck to King Richard!*
The joy-bells are ringing
All over the town.
Bolingbroke's banished,
The rebel has vanished,
Richard is up,
And Bolingbroke's down!

Bow down your head,
King Richard the Second!
Bow down your head
And put off the crown!
The people are wailing
*Bad luck to King Richard!*

And mock at him trailing
His chains through the town.
His dog as he lingers
Licks Bolingbroke's fingers,
Bolingbroke's up,
And Richard is down!

# *Henry IV*
## 1399

BOLINGBROKE, Bolingbroke, what will you do?
The Kingdom of England is split into two!

Harry the Hotspur, the flame of the North,
Is chafing to vanquish you, Henry the Fourth!

Douglas of Scotland is arming his clans
To fight you and beat you and baffle your plans!

Owen Glendower, the wizard of Wales,
Is marshalling demons and devils with tails!

Richard's poor zany, a wandering elf,
Is claiming, men say, to be Richard himself!

And Harry, your son, sits in taverns and sings,
And cares not a straw for the glory of kings!

Bolingbroke, Bolingbroke, what will you do? –
'I'll do a king's duty and see the thing through!

'I'll show this young Hotspur, so bristling and bold,
What happens to lords who don't do what they're
    told!

'I'll strike at the Douglas who scoffs at my sway
And slit up his bagpipe for ever and aye!

'Glendower in Wales I'll besiege and beset –
I was never afraid of a bogeyman yet!

'The wandering zany is nothing to dread –
Let him say what he chooses, King Richard is dead!

'And my son, who has driven a thorn through my
    heart,
Will learn in good season to take the King's part!'

## Henry V
## 1413

HENRY was a wild boy,
    Fond of fun and fooling;
When he was the Prince of Wales
    He made a hash of schooling;
Rollicking with tosspots,
    Trying daddy's crown on,
Henry was the sort of boy
    Fathers always frown on.

Henry was a brave man,
    Fond of martial phrases;
When he was the English King
    He won his country's praises;
Bucking up his soldiers,
    Urging rank and file on,
Henry was the sort of man
    Women always smile on.

## *Henry VI*
## 1422

CONSIDERING Henry
The Sixth wasn't strong,
It's very surprising
He lasted so long;
At the age of nine months
He came into his own,
And for thirty-nine years
Kept his seat on the throne.
He had troubles in France
With Orleans' fair Maid,
And troubles at home
With the rebel Jack Cade,
But the worst of his troubles,
As everyone knows,
Was the war that was waged
Twixt the Red and White Rose.

At St Albans they fought,
And the White won the field;
Then they fought at Bloreheath,
Where the Red had to yield;
At Wakefield the White
Had to swallow a loss,
But won at Northampton
And Mortimer's Cross;
Then back in St Albans
They battled again,
And this time the Red
Carried off the campaign;
Till at Towton soon after,
One day in the spring,
The White turned the tables
And captured the King.

Then Lancaster sank
Like a plummet of lead,
Singing 'Oh, for the Red Rose!
The Red Rose is dead!'
While the Yorkists as buoyant
And bobbish as corks,
Sang 'Hey, for the White Rose!
The White Rose of Yorks!'
So Henry the Sixth
Had to take a back seat
With his higgledy-piggledy
Men in retreat,
And although at this point
His unhappy reign closes,
They *still* went on fighting
The Wars of the Roses!

## Edward IV
# 1461

KING EDWARD THE FOURTH was
gay,
King Edward the Fourth was charming,
 He'd a voice like silk,
 And manners like milk,
And a smile that was most disarming.

King Edward the Fourth was vexed
By the Duke of Clarence, his brother,
 Although they had
 The selfsame dad
As well as the selfsame mother.

King Edward the Fourth was harsh,
So without any pangs or qualms he
 Upsided-downed
 His brother and drowned
Him dead in a butt of malmsey.

King Edward the Fourth was gay,
King Edward the Fourth was charming,
  He'd a voice like silk,
  And manners like milk,
And a smile that was most disarming.

# *Edward V*
## 1483

EDWARD THE FIRST was the one that was tall,
Edward the Second was weakest of all,
Edward the Third was the first in the fray,
Edward the Fourth the most gallant and gay –
And Edward the Fifth was a nice little lad
Who never grew up to be good or be bad.

He might have been taller than Edward the First,
Like Edward the Second, he might have been worst,
He might have been braver than Edward the Third,
Or than Edward the Fourth a more debonair bird –
But what Edward the Fifth would have been as a man,
Well, nobody knows, because nobody can.

Alas for this nice little, poor little lad!
His reign was the shortest that any king had –
And if, gentle reader, you want to know why,
Turn to Richard the Third, and you'll find the reply.

## *Richard III*
## 1483

CROOKBACK DICK
    Had nephews two,
Younger than me,
    Older than you.

Crookback Dick,
    He spoke them fair,
One was king,
    The other was heir.

Crookback Dick,
    He longed for power,
So he smothered his nephews
    In the Tower.

Nobody dared
    To say a word,
And Crookback Dick
    Became Richard the Third.

## Henry VII
## 1485

LAMBERT SIMNEL
    Why do you sit
In the King's kitchen
    Turning the spit?
'Alas! I aspired
    To the throne in my youth,
And said I was Warwick,
    Which wasn't the truth.
But Henry the Seventh
At Stoke overcame me,
And made me, to shame me,
    The turnspit you see –
And as the joints sizzle,
I sit and I grizzle
And think of the fizzle
    That came of my spree!'

Perkin Warbeck
    Why do you glower
Out of the window
    In the King's Tower?

'Alas! In my folly
    I rose up at Cork
And said I was Richard,
    The young Duke of York.
But Henry the Seventh
Pursued me to Beaulieu,
And shut me up duly
    To ponder my lot
And dream of the chopper
Which monarchs think proper
To put as a stopper
    On people who plot!'

## *Henry VIII*
## 1509

BLUFF KING HAL was full of beans;
He married half a dozen queens;
For three called Kate they cried the banns,
And one called Jane, and a couple of Annes.

The first he asked to share his reign
Was Kate of Aragon, straight from Spain –
But when his love for her was spent,
He got a divorce, and out she went.

Anne Boleyn was his second wife;
He swore to cherish her all his life –
But seeing a third he wished instead,
He chopped off poor Anne Boleyn's head.

He married the next afternoon
Jane Seymour, which was rather soon –
But after one year as his bride
She crept into her bed and died.

Anne of Cleves was Number Four;
Her portrait thrilled him to the core –
But when he met her face to face
Another royal divorce took place.

Catherine Howard, Number Five,
Billed and cooed to keep alive –
But one day Henry felt depressed;
The executioner did the rest.

Sixth and last came Catherine Parr,
Sixth and last and luckiest far –
For this time it was Henry who
Hopped the twig, and a good job too.

## Edward VI
## 1547

EDWARD THE SIXTH made little noise,
And died ere he was old;
He loved books better than his toys,
Or so I have been told;
And all through him the Bluecoat Boys
Still go in legs of gold.

# Mary
## 1553

WHEN Mary wore the English crown,
Old England still held Calais Town,
But ere she died, to Mary's pain,
Old France got Calais back again.

Now, for some cause obscure and queer,
Mary held Calais far more dear
Than all the charming English towns
Between the Cheviots and the Downs.

'Alas!' quoth she to those who tried
To soothe her grief and heal her pride,
'You'll find when I this life depart
*Calais* engraved upon my heart!'

A truly touching thought – but who
Could say for sure if it was true,
Since no one in those Tudor days
Had yet discovered the X-rays?

## *Elizabeth I*
## 1558

HAIL, Queen Elizabeth! Here comes Queen Bess
In a very big ruff and a very wide dress;
Her hair it is red, and her eyes they are green,
And England has prospered since Bess became Queen.

The boldest of sailors have sailed to the West,
The greatest of poets have written their best,
The gayest of people have danced on the green,
And England's grown merry since Bess became Queen.

She's vain as a peacock that opens its tail,
She's proud as an eagle that weathers the gale,
She's crafty and jealous, suspicious and mean,
But England is England now Bess is the Queen.

## *James I*
## 1603

JAMES THE FIRST is now the king
I'll help you in remembering.

Please remember James was not
An English monarch, but a Scot.

Also, James had goggle eyes,
And drank more liquor than was wise.

James the First it was who sold
Titles in return for gold.

Furthermore, he took a pride
In hunting, though he couldn't ride.

But if James the First you'd fix
So that in your mind he sticks,

Then remember, in his reign,
Guy Fawkes tried, and tried in vain,

With gunpowder to explode
The Parliamentary abode.

So, my child, when you and I,
Lighting fireworks, think of Guy,

Let us, mid the pretty flames,
Remember to remember James.

## *Charles I*
# 1625

KING CHARLES he was a gentleman
    Who wore the finest suits,
With scented gloves upon his hands
    And lace upon his boots.
His hat it had the widest brim
    And very longest feather,
And in a golden barge he sailed
    The Thames in summer weather.

King Charles was such a gentleman
    He couldn't rule the land,
For all the lace upon his boot
    And perfume on his hand.
Alas, alas, his wide-brimmed hat!
    Alas, his sweeping feather!
King Charles he lost both hat and head
    One winter day together

## Oliver Cromwell
## 1653

DOWN with actors! Down with plays!
Such the cry in Cromwell's days!
Down with puppets! Down with sport!
Down with fun of every sort!
Tightrope-walking, football, cricket,
Even bowls is counted wicked!
England's governed by objectors!
Lord protect us from Protectors!

Now are jesters all suppressed!
Cap and bells must take a rest!
No more wrestling on the green
Or grinning matches now are seen!
Now the merry maypole's hidden!
Christmas puddings are forbidden!
Oh, these circumspect inspectors!
Lord protect us from Protectors!

# Charles II
## 1660

PRETTY Nell Gwynne of Drury Lane
  Crying Sweet Oranges in the rain,
Whom do you sell to?
                    'Any who'll buy,
Tom, Dick, or Harry, for what care I?
But the ripest orange of all I'll bring
To lay in the hand of Charles the King.'

Pretty Nell Gwynne on the stage tonight
With your cartwheel hat and your smile so bright,
Whom do you sing to?
                    'Any who'll pay,
Tom, Dick, or Harry, to see the play –
But the merriest song of all I'll sing
In the royal ear of Charles the King.'

Pretty Nell Gwynne in your palace grand,
As by the window you take your stand,
Whom do you wait for?
                    'Any who'll call,
Tom, Dick, or Harry, I'll kiss them all,
Yes, all shall be welcome as flowers in spring,
But I'll keep my best kiss for Charles the King.'

Merry Charles Stuart, now death is near,

When sick men hope, or believe, or fear,
Whom do you pray for?
                    'Prayer is vain,
Yet this I'll pray in my dying pain –
Pray take poor Nelly my golden ring,
And let her not starve,' said Charles the King.

## *James II*
## 1685

FOUR Stuart kings there were, whose names
Were James and Charles and Charles and James.

The first, as history makes plain,
Was ugly, greedy, gross, and vain.

The second, it must be allowed,
Was dense, pernickety, and proud.

The third, if I make no mistake,
Was an incorrigible rake.

The fourth combined, it seems to me,
The vices of the other three.

So England cried, 'Avaunt! No more
These Scottish Stuarts we'll adore,

But try instead a monarch much
Safer, if stodgier, from the Dutch.'

So Orange William hove in sight,
And James the Second took to flight.

No Stuart King has since been known
To sit upon the English throne.

But though in practice they were not
A very efficacious lot,

They still look well in picture frames,
Do James and Charles and Charles and James.

### *William and Mary*
## 1689

WILLIAM AND MARY
They sat on one throne;
You can't think of one
Of the couple alone.
How seldom we've heard
Of William the Third!
How rarely we've reckoned
With Mary the Second!
But William and Mary
Are known to the many
Like two indivisible
Sides of a penny,
And stick in the histories,
One by the other,
As close as a Siamese
Twin to his brother.

## Anne
## 1702

QUEEN ANNE's dead!
Poor Queen Anne!
If she was plain,
She had a pretty fan,
If she was dull,
She wore a pretty gown,
And almost looked alive
Underneath her crown.

Queen Anne's dead!
Poor plain Anne!
Fold her pretty gown,
Close her pretty fan,
And on her pretty monument
Let nothing else be read
But these plain words:
Queen Anne's dead!

## George I
# 1714

GEORGE THE FIRST, when he was young,
Couldn't speak the English tongue;
In Hanover, where he was born,
He spoke in German night and morn.

George, George, with a rum-tum-tum
An English deputation's come!
Go and greet it where it waits! –
George went in and said *Wie geht's?*

George, George, in England they
Want you for their king today!
Say you will, with heart and soul! –
George, delighted, said *Jawohl!*

George the First, till he was dead,
Still his prayers in German said.
Wasn't that a funny thing
For one who was an English king?

## George II
### 1727

THE SECOND GEORGE in England rules
   With heavy pomp and splendour –
Yet still there are romantic fools
   Who love the Young Pretender.
And it's 'Come, Charlie, come, with fife and drum,
   Come back to your lawful islands!
There are soldiers who will give their lives for you,
   A-passing round the watchword in the Highlands.'

The Second George sits down to dine
   And swill the British barley,
While many a secret toast in wine
   Is tossed to Gay Prince Charlie.
And it's 'Strike, Charlie, strike, with gun and pike,
   Strike now for your lawful islands!
This Georgie-Porge we will make disgorge
   His dinner when he meets us in the Highlands.'

The Second George his Army sends
   To Scotland damp and sodden,
And they smash the Young Pretender's friends
   To pieces at Culloden.
And it's 'Run, Charlie, run, your day is done,
   Take ship for the nearest islands!
If you are wise, you will don a good disguise,
   And never, never come back to the Highlands!'

# George III
## 1760

THEY called this King the Farmer,
    And two fine farms had he;
His little farm was England,
    The land of you and me,
His big was North America
Where George the Third made much more hay.

They called this King the Farmer,
    So fond was he of sheep
He thought about them waking
    And counted them in sleep;
In fact, he filled his thoughts with wool
Until he got his noddle full.

They called this King the Farmer.
    So ill he farmed, they say,
That a Yankee called George Washington
    Declared one July day:
'America has had about
Enough of Kings – we'll turn 'em out!'

They called this King the Farmer.
   The ways of sheep he knew,
But what will do for woolly lambs
   For men will never do;
So England had to pay the cost,
And George's biggest farm was lost.

## *George IV*
## 1820

KING GEORGE THE FOURTH is vain and fat
    And fond of shirts with frills,
And keeps his tradesmen on the mat
    When they send in their bills;
He borrows money from the Jews
    On every rainy day,
And when they dun him for their dues,
    The Country has to pay.

King George the Fourth, he often goes
    To Brighton for a spree,
Where all the bucks and all the beaux
    Parade beside the sea;
They quiz the girls with stare serene
    As they go tripping by,
And even Georgie has been seen
    To wink a regal eye.

# *William IV*
# 1830

YO HO HO, my hearties!
  Hark! The seamen sing!
   With a bottle of rum
   For Will-i-um
The Fourth, our Sailor King!

Set him in the crow's nest,
A spyglass to his eye,
   And there ain't no brig,
   Be she little or big,
Will pass our William by!

Set him in the cockpit,
A noggin in his hand,
   And there ain't no tar
   More pop-u-lar
On the sea or the dry, dry land!

Yo ho ho, my hearties!
So the seamen sing!
   With a loud hoorah
   For Brittany-anny-ah
Now Willy-illy-um is king!

# *Victoria*
## 1837

VICTORIA, Victoria,
  Was England's pride and joy
When grandma was a baby
And grandpa was a boy,
And they can still remember
The happy days long fled,
When the penny stamp was purple
And the ha'penny stamp was red.

Then Salisbury and Gladstone
Were powers in the land,
And Dickens was an idol,
And the Albert Hall was grand;
And hostesses resorted
To Gunter's for a spread,
When the penny stamp was purple
And the ha'penny stamp was red.

Then saucy Nellie Farren
Was billed upon the boards,
And Grace sat in a growler
And bundled down to Lords,
And everyone repeated
What Mr Whistler said,
When the penny stamp was purple
And the ha'penny stamp was red.

Then Wolseley or whoever
Went forth to fight our foes
Was honoured by Lord Tennyson
As well as by Tussaud's,
And Watts and Ouida were alive
And Darwin wasn't dead,
When the penny stamp was purple
And the ha'penny stamp was red.

Now the penny stamp is scarlet
And the ha'penny stamp is green – *
How different from the days when Queen
Victoria was queen;
The far-off days when grandpapa
And grandmamma were wed,
And the penny stamp was purple
And the ha'penny stamp was red!

*1 Till 1951 A.D.
This chronicle rang true –
Then the ha'penny stamp turned orange
And the penny stamp turned blue.

Now the ha'penny stamp is blue
And the penny stamp maroon
But that is all too likely
To be altered very soon.

## Edward VII
## 1901

KING EDWARD was a peace-maker
    Whenever he'd a chance,
He kept the peace with Germany,
    He kept the peace with France.

King Edward he liked horse-racing
    As much as humbler folks,
He'd something on the Derby
    And he'd something on the Oaks.

King Edward wore a Homburg hat
    And went to Homburg Spa,
And when he was the Prince of Wales
    Was scared of his mamma.

## George V
# 1910

G EORGE THE FIFTH had a naval beard,
Was far more loved than he was feared,
And when in public he appeared
Was cheered and cheered and cheered and cheered.

He sat upon the throne before
The War we fought to finish War,
And when at last the War was o'er
He sat upon the throne some more.

Of kings he was the first who stirred
His subjects with the spoken word,
Because before his voice was heard
The BBC had not occurred.

He broadcast in a friendly way,
And almost everyone would stay
At home to hear what he would say,
Especially on Christmas Day.

# *Edward VIII*
## 1936

HE started as the Prince of Wales,
For that's how kings begin, sir,
But here is a peculiar thing!
Of all the kings of whom we sing,
He was the one and only king
To end as Duke of Windsor.

As Prince he won the People's hearts
From John o'Groat's to Dover;
He hated pomp, he hated pride,
He travelled far, he travelled wide,
And fought in the War on the winning side,
And danced when it was over.

As King the dressing-up and fuss
Upon his feelings grated;
He could not manage to forget
The lady whom they would not let
Him marry to his great regret,
And so he abdicated.

For while he led one kind of life,
He longed to lead another;
He told us on the microphone
He could not bear to live alone –
And so for love he left his throne
And gave it to his brother.

He ended up as Windsor's Duke
In English History's tale, sir,
Which is a most unusual thing
Among the kings of whom we sing,
For *they* all ended up as king
When they started as Prince of Wales, sir.

# *George VI*
## 1936

HE was the Campers' King,
    The best of Scouts was he,
He liked to joke and sing
    And join the Jamboree.

He did not think to reign;
    With family and wife
He thought to live the plain
    Englishman's homely life.

But life itself said, 'No!
    England is your dower,
And you with her must go
    Through her darkest hour.'

Unfaltering he bore
    Through six disastrous years
The Jamboree of War
    And blood and sweat and tears.

The Peace that was no peace
    Still saw him at the helm
Labouring without cease
    For his ravaged realm.

When sickness stole his breath
    He spared himself no less –
Then, overnight, came death
    With gentle suddenness.

Until his time ran out
    Duty was his creed;
Say of this Royal Scout:
    'His Life was his Good Deed.'

## *Elizabeth II*
## 1952

SO the queens come: and so the kings go,
And what they were like we shall never quite know,
Till history's mystery comes to a close,
And here is the Queen that everyone knows.

'Roger McGough is a true original and more than
one generation would be much the poorer without
him' – *The Times Educational Supplement*

'. . . A collection that works well on the page
and is a delight to read aloud' – *Guardian*

'Very silly, utterly crazy humour'
– Jeremy Strong, *Guardian*

Full of Brian Patten's wonderful wit!

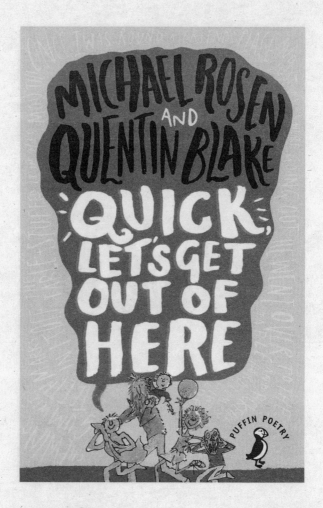

'Michael Rosen is one of our most popular writers
– the champion for every bored, overdrilled,
tested-to-tears pupil in the land' – *The Times*

# It all started with a Scarecrow

**Puffin is over seventy years old.**
Sounds ancient, doesn't it? But Puffin has never been
so lively. We're always on the lookout for the next big
idea, which is how it began all those years ago.

Penguin Books was a big idea from the mind of
a man called Allen Lane, who in 1935 invented
the quality paperback and changed the world.
**And from great Penguins, great Puffins grew,
changing the face of children's books forever.**

The first four Puffin Picture Books were hatched in 1940 and the
first Puffin story book featured a man with broomstick arms called
Worzel Gummidge. In 1967 Kaye Webb, Puffin Editor, started the
Puffin Club, promising to **'make children into readers'**.
She kept that promise and over 200,000 children became devoted
Puffineers through their quarterly instalments of *Puffin Post*.

Many years from now, we hope you'll look back and
remember Puffin with a smile. **No matter what your age
or what you're into, there's a Puffin for everyone.**
The possibilities are endless, but one thing is for sure:
whether it's a picture book or a paperback, a sticker book
or a hardback, **if it's got that little Puffin
on it – it's bound to be good.**

**www.puffinbooks.com**